TO KEEP YOU IN THIS WORLD

To Keep You in This World

POEMS

ANN CALANDRO

SERVING HOUSE BOOKS

To Keep You in This World
Copyright © 2026 Ann Calandro
First Edition

All rights reserved. No part of this book may be reproduced or transmitted in any form or by any means, electronic, digital, or mechanical, including photocopy, audio recording, or any information storage and retrieval system, without prior permission from the publisher or author (except by reviewers who may quote brief passages). No part of this book may be used or reproduced in any manner for the purpose of training artificial intelligence technologies or systems.

Paperback ISBN: 9781947175761

Cover art: "Transitopia" by Ann Calandro, originally published in *Lumina Journal,* Spring/Summer 2024

Cover design by Jacob Arms

Published by Serving House Books
Lawrence Landing Company
Raleigh, North Carolina 27609
United States of America

www.servinghousebooks.com

Serving House Books is a proud member of

Independent Book Publishers Association
and
Community of Literary Magazines and Presses

SERVING HOUSE BOOKS

In memory of my parents

CONTENTS

Beginnings	1
High Sail	2
Nightmare	3
Road Rage	4
Cheers	5
Summer	6
Small Wars	7
Breakfast	8
The Cutting Board	9
The Patio	10
Winter Day	11
Gestures	12
Miles	13
On the Roof	15
Winter's Wounds	16
Mistress Hopkins	17
A Day of Hearts	19
Clocks and Hearts	20
Dream Practice	21
Dream House	22
Asleep	24
No Words	26
Thanksgiving	27
The Closets	28
Hands	29
Idling	30
Laundry	31
Lecture	32
Footnote	33

Obscene Phone Call	34
Portrait of a Kelly Girl...	35
Have a Good Day	38
Prelude	40
Hopeful	41
Love Poem	43
Morning Colors	44
Return Migration	45
Don't Eat the Chicken	47
Gratis	49
Toward the End	50
Shadow Child	51
Photograph of a Friend	52
Plate-Cup- Bowl	53
On Being Yellow	54
Dear Jerry	55
Contour Drawing	57
On the Hill	58
Touched Wood	59
Reconstitution	60
Transformations	61
Typing Papers	62
Upstate Spring	63
Verbal Silences	64
Where the Kissing Never...	65
Greensleeves	66
A Walnut Tree	67
Midas in his Attic Room	69
Into the City	70
I Haven't Thought of You	73
To Keep You in This World	77
Answers	80

Consigned	81
The Memory Box	82
All That Time	84
Water	86
Tee Shirts	87
A Memory I Didn't Know	89
Step Inside with Me	90
Fault	91
Concert	93
The Minor Keys	94
The Goodbye Waltz	96
Roots	97
Acknowledgements	99
Credits	100
About the Author	101

Beginnings

It would be simpler now to doubt
That cold will stop, simpler
To live forever sick
In our bleaker selves,
Simpler that crops lie crippled in the soil,
Crushed by frost for trusting spring to stir,
But through this bitter winter I still hope
For warmth, for a small
Jagged burst of green, for mercy
That winter will not last
Forever.

High Sail

There are months
Of high sail, blue breeze,
And the clean snap
As day climbs into bed with you,
Shutting off the light until morning
Parts your eyes.

One night loss crawls
in with you instead,
Grunting, barking,
Whimpering in your arms,
Knotting the sheets until morning
Stings your heart.

Nightmare

I wake to find myself
Asleep, bent sharp as a ship's prow
Against a woolen sea. Dreaming,
I row harshly,
Breasting steep waves
Between night and day.
Fish skeletons crust my eyes.
My arms fly up, cresting blue sheets.
My face turns cardboard, smudged with gray,
Pulse seeping to the reddening heart of dawn.
I thrash to wake, not capsize
Into tears, to be reborn.

Road Rage

Eyes smashed
Wet with crystal
Tears, skull
Crushed, nose
Buried in a chrome
Elbow, through
No fault
Of its own.

Cheers

Morning ruffles my hair
With cold fingers.
When I don't respond,
She lights a cigarette
Behind my eyes.

Those days I can't
Get out of bed.
My mind won't walk.
My heart won't breathe.
I pull what I will do
And have done
At some other time
In some other place
Up to my chin.

Morning sprawls
On my skull
And agitates the bone.
If I stagger to the kitchen
I want coffee
That goes down like voltage.

Summer

The days fry up fast here,
Butterscorched in brick and asphalt,
Topped with a slice of melting blue
That drips and congeals.

People hollow out here
Into rough-scooped melon shells
Tossed from the stoops,
Sucked dry and scraped raw.

Small Wars

Each minute pulls
At my sleeve. I burn
Eggs and toast, boil
Coffee and myself.

Morning keeps me
Company, a friendly pest
Who won't let me escape
For days.

Breakfast

The mornings are mountains
I'm tired of climbing.
At their peaks
Are scrambled news,
The crusted corners of burnt dreams,
And fresh-brewed outrage.
We drink mugs of it each day.
What happened? Who stopped listening
To reason? Smashing people's lives
Down on the kitchen table
May feel good to someone,
But doing so solves nothing.

The Cutting Board

I chop fruit
On an old cutting board.

Juice and pulp spew
Over my hands.

They dull and thicken.
I dump the garbage.

The slices I save--
Letters, photos,

Promises cracked like bones
And stuffed into the bulge of years--

Wait for the pick-up man
Who never comes.

The Patio

After the last
Move, I told you

To bury me
Under the patio

So that I would never
Have to move again.

That was a joke.
What was true was that

I thought I'd grow older
And you would stay

The same.
I'm older now, older than you

Ever were, and you are gone.
The patio remains.

Winter Day

Three steps into the day
I pull it over me.

Wind hunches on my collar,
Drools down my back.

Slabs of street
Shiver under asphalt.

Even the sun is frozen,
Hiding in an unheated sky.

Cinder
In a cold blue eye.

With an ungloved hand, I pack my mind
Inside my pocket.

Gestures

I will live alone, in a solitary gap
without greetings or final hugs, all
gestures for those who come and leave
discarded, left in another time.

Our friends quicken summer into fall
and hang us madly between joy and grief.
To wade memory is to sound pain's floor.
I will live alone, perhaps.

Miles

Each morning
I put on sneakers, pin my keys inside
My pocket, walk left
Out the door and left again
At the corner, then a mile or more straight
To the outskirts of town, to the abandoned
Gas station's buckling pavement and
Waist-high weeds. Then right
And right again across the tracks,
Along what becomes
Main Street, its Victorian ladies opening
Their shutters, stretching a flagpole, beginning
To stir.

I've walked miles for years. I looked and planned
For that paint, this brick, those flowers, this tile,
That life. Later I walked as a camera,
My eyes scanning, heart pumping,
Legs moving smoothly, my mind detached.
Don't you agree
It's better that way?

At the news agent, where I buy the daily paper
And treat myself to fresh iced coffee with lots
Of milk, I exchange smiles
With the courteous owner.
Sometimes he gives me a cup
Of cold water. "Drink this," he commands,
And I do. Then I'm walking, turning right

At the 5 and Dime, a quick left
At the paint store, another right, and I'm back
On my street, facing east.
Once I timed it
Just right
To see the sun rising,
But since then I've always been
Too early, or too late.

On the Roof

At first I wished
I could have seen you

Balanced on your roof
Some 20 feet above

The quiet morning,
In a picture that my child

Might draw: pale house, bright sun,
Blue sky, green lawn,

Your hands removing
And replacing tile.

I drove by too late
And you were gone.

Where the ladder stood,
A shadow slanted down.

The new roof glowed, caught
In the evening sun.

Someone honked, and I drove on.
You were always out of reach.

Winter's Wounds

Yesterday
Winter's wounds
Opened

And bled away
Last year's
Gray cracked

Skin of snow
Until
The raw new earth

Uncurled
Between fists
Of frozen grass.

Today
All is stretched
And tender,

The ground's
Soaked fringe
Of bitter green

Anoints the air
With a smell
Of dill.

Mistress Hopkins

>13 April 1642. The governor of Hartford brought his wife with him, a godly young woman and of special parts, who had fallen into a sad infirmity [through] reading and writing.

I walk a careful day
Between the household
and my sons, stitching
Cloth, churning cream.
Cold, I sink
From one task to
Another, drowning
My vocation like a cat.

>If she had attended her household affairs, she [would] have kept her wits.

These are bitter yellow days
When the world is so
Out of focus
I cannot commit it
To paper.
The back room holds
The desk I haven't used
Since summer. Since we've moved
To do God's work
I have no time
For my own, though I do not begrudge
Edward and the boys my hands

Or heart.

        Such things as belong to women.

God finds me worn down
Almost to the spirit.

        Out of her way from the place God had set her.

Still, he listens to my heart
And not my words,
And even the world is
Not so black as I paint it
In this long sickness
My life.

Behind the wife another woman
Cracks in a new April, fleeing
Her small town,
Her scattered life.

A Day of Hearts

They're stamping out hearts,
Selling them by the dozens;
Perfect, indestructible, glazed sweet red
Hollow hearts,
Guaranteed replaceable
At a low, low price.
I have one:
Damaged,
Not replaceable;
The price is right.
It should be careful
Whom it loves,
Being otherwise imperfect.

Clocks and Hearts

for Jim, 1953-1983

Morning, and I grope
For darkness, eyes shut
Against the howl
Of hours. They pull me
Toward one more day
Like all the others.

Encircled
By the hands
That propel me,
I foot the hours
And knows
There is cause
For alarm.

The clock carves on,
Slicing the day
Into ribbons.

I savor frozen moments,
Like the day
You came running with a rose,
As if the next second
Would shear the petals
From your hand.

Dream Practice

At 10 p.m.
We check our morals
With our coats
And watch possibility
Blow us a kiss.

Here we are careful
To do everything
By accident: shrugging off the day,
Bumping the night
Between our hips,
And snapping qualms
Off our fingers.

At 4 a.m.
The bar folds
Into morning.
We reclaim our coats,
Make change to pay,
And stop spilling our dreams
Into practice.

Dream House

Don't we all have a dream
House? It's the perfect house we thought
We'd never find, but one day there
It is, a miracle, caught in the glue
Of listings or in the bloodshot corner
Of your eye as you whiz past.
My dream house arrived
In a message from the realtor.
I clicked on its bright blue siding, hidden
By trees that leaned over
Its shingled roof, and saw precisely
What I want—to be hidden
By fence and foliage and still
Around the corner from the ordinary world
Of asphalt and groceries. I lust after
The plant-filled sunroom, the tiny bathroom
Tiles of black and white, the tucked-away heartbeat
Of a dead-end street
Near whispering traffic. I will sit
On the golden deck under rustling trees,
Leaves in my hair, early morning
Coffee in my hand, joyful birds singing
Hallelujah.

Hallelujah? Not so fast.
The roof is twenty-five years old,
The amperage not up to code,
The asking price too high,
The carpets badly stained with tea or piss.

No one knows
What's underneath.
The moldy basement is unfinished,
The bedrooms dollhouse small.
There's only one shower
And not enough closets.
I'm too tired for this house
To be my dream.
I owned a yellow Cape Cod once
And fled it for a condo, vowing
Never to go back to a life
Of raking and repair.
I gave that house my heart and wallet
For sixteen endless years, and still it turned
Its back on me each day.

No, I'll stay here with my coffee, syllables
On the tiny table, meter tapping its fork
Against my plate. I'll feed myself
A poem, not a house or a dream.
Farewell, dream house, glowing sapphire blue.
Already I miss you, and we never met.

Asleep

Asleep I hold an ancient map.
I unfold you, trace
Every line, linger
At each junction,
Splice your heart
To mine.

Awake you walked away
To someone else, refused me
One last kiss, never said
Good-bye.

Dreaming, pinioned
At the border of memory
And desire, I wander
Your voice, travel
Your smile, hike
Your hands. My heart
Spikes and surges.
I fall back through the years
To reach your arms, to be unhooked,
Unbuttoned, and undone.
The night is drenched with morning sun,
All sounds are silenced, our whereabouts unknown.
For one sun-soaked minute
Time stops, resumes more slowly.
Do you know how dear
You were to me?

Asleep, we get up,
Brush off soft crumbs of guilt and regret,
Refold the map, prepare to go.
You stayed young but I am old.
No one will know, we say without words.
No one gets hurt.

I walk to a car that isn't mine
And drive home on unfamiliar roads,
Passing through someone's life
Like any commuter,
While inside me
Arpeggios unfurl.

Asleep, I held an ancient map of you.
I unfolded you, traced
Every line, lingered
At each junction,
Spliced your heart
To mine.

No Words

No words describe the place
Where one color meets another,

Where purple soothes and comforts gray,
Where fiery brick crumbles into red.

No word explains those times
When the life we live

And the life we dream
Collide

At inconvenient minutes
In unexpected places,

While your fingers tease open
The small buttons on my sweater

That the cashier called haze
But to me is air.

Thanksgiving

for my aunt

We deal you pills like gamblers,
past hope of recovery or fear of death;
pills that bloat your face and make you wake
enough to cry when anyone comes near.

You sleep. We carve a solemn turkey, pass plates
around the broken circle, give thanks where
there is none to give, sit curved and scalloped
near your bed.

As a child I flew to visit you
in California, the magical place
where fruit as clean and hard
as golf balls hung from every tree,
and blue waves bit white sand.

Your home was bright loud fun:
blenders tumbled carrots into juice,
forks fell gracefully upon the floor.
Here you lie in yellow silence, wet with fever, until
death comes to eat your heart for breakfast.

And though the doctors sucked like gnats
at your cancer, it was not enough.
It is never enough.
Back at college, I open the letter
from home, already knowing
you are dead.

The Closets

Last night
Two bottles of wine
Climbed into the linens,
One shelf below.

This morning
My children's report cards
Scatter their lies and promises
Among the shirts.

Postcards are writing
To each other, realizing
They will never leave
This house.

There have been skirmishes
Between the screwdrivers.
My shoes refuse
To leave their boxes.

The closets bulge,
As if with mumps.
I won't carry this poem outside.
It could be dangerous.

Hands

Our hands accept the mundane
Tasks that get us through
Each day: chopping onions,
Tying shoes on feet
That walk straight
Uncomplicated blocks,
Leaving the mind free
To wander through its land-
Locked waves.

Our hands accept us
When we don't accept
Ourselves: brushing hair,
Guiding arms to spoons and coins,
Tucking us under
Other hands we want
To touch, and telling us we haven't turned
Too desperate, too loathsome,
Or too scared.

Hands accept
The thankless task
Of thanking themselves:
Picking up a pen to write
Thank you
While we hope that
Real thanks comes along.

Idling

Soon
Our friendship
Will run on ink

And at night
I will funnel
The day
Into words

And mail them
To you
While my heart
Pumps its wish

That you stand
Idling
On the edges
Of my day

Laundry

Fluorescent lights
Scour my shadow,
Finger-cold on porcelain,

While I hold wet sheets
Wrung out like days.

Bright wads churn
In a frantic circle dance,
Thawing into towels.

A sleeve surfaces,
Waving languidly,
And is captured by its partner.

I join socks,
Press pants and shirts together
Into domes of color—

heaping pieces of my life
Into one soft pile
To swing across my shoulders.

Lecture

No sounds
But the cracking
Of knuckles and the crisping
Of paper passing
From hand to desk
Through squares of polished sun

The voice begins
Threading words through
Breeze and light
And twitching feet
Dreaming under chairs

Words pour down his chin
Collect in puddles
Collar on his breastbone
Missing our ears

Footnote

for my editor and proofreader friends

Words are bored
Standing at attention
Twenty-four hours a day.
They would prefer to slouch
Against each other,
Nap a bit,
Have a beer or two,
Wash off the touch of mind.

They outline
Their battle plans:
Seizing our desks,
Deleting us,
Committing criticism.

After the revolution
They red-pencil us
Out of existence.

Obscene Phone Call

Like us all, she craves
The rustle of newspaper
And cornflakes,
Lacks the quick kiss,
The misplaced glove,

Prepares her meals and listens
To the forecast
With half an ear
While she waits alone
For the 8:02.

She clasps her own hands
Over the morning and hears
The roar
Of an approaching train.

Once, she answered
The startled phone
and heard nothing
But breath, nothing
But some other human
Breath in her palm, searching
For a small portion
Of touch and sound.

Portrait of a Kelly Girl At Lunch

One summer I was what was called
A Kelly Girl, between junior and senior year
Of high school, although the company
That hired me wasn't Kelly.
It had another name
I can't remember.
All summer long
I worked one week
Here, another week there, always
Filing papers, answering calls,
Retrieving pens and pads
From the storage room, wearing
Old-lady skirts with pinching waists,
Collared shirts that bothered my neck,
Pointy shoes with slippery soles,
And worst of all: stockings.
At home I'd dive into frayed jeans
And peasant blouses, put Joni Mitchell
On the stereo, and loudly sing along.

On my last day, the man I report to
Invites me out to lunch "for a job
Well done," and I accept. I am tired
Of my brown-bag lunches
That wilt in the heat.
"Yes, thank you," I say.
At noon he comes to my desk
And we walk to a nearby restaurant
With white tablecloths

And waiters who pause often
To pour ice water slowly, without a smile.
"This is nice," I say, trying to eat
More neatly. It's a complicated
Sandwich that's hard to hold,
But it tastes wonderful. I feel grown-up,
Chewing delicately, dabbing my mouth
With a thick cloth napkin.
"My wife and I have an arrangement,"
Says the man. My blank look shows him
I don't understand what he means.
He explains that he and his wife are free
To sleep with other people,
And that right now she is sleeping
With a young man in her office.
"At this very moment?" I ask, confused.
"Well, probably not at this exact moment,"
He laughs. "But you get the picture,
And I tell you this
Because I would like to sleep with you."
I don't know what to say except an astonished no.
He's old, maybe even thirty,
With receding hair, and I'm seventeen.
In those days, maybe this happens all the time,
Like the whistles from construction workers
And the men pressing against your back
On the subway, but this is the first time
It has happened to me.
"I just want a dessert, please," I say
As a platter of petit-fours passes by
On the arm of a waiter.
The man beckons the waiter.

"A few for the lady," he orders.
To me he says, "Don't bother
Coming back to the office. Don't worry,
We'll mail your check to you. Go on home."
He throws bills on the table and leaves,
Shaking his head as if I have made
A terrible mistake. How can he know
That I am waiting for love,
For romance, for all the dewy boys
I imagine, for all the words
And worlds in the songs.
Right now I am happy to be excused,
Left alone to eat a plate
Of pastries for free before returning
Home, to my teenage dreams.

Have a Good Day

At the chilly supermarket, loud and bright,
I dread the inevitable
Question from the cashier:
"How are you?"
What can I say?
No one wants a truthful answer.
This is America.
The question is a placeholder.
"Great, thanks," I say. "And you?
"Fine, thanks."
The groceries begin their tumbled journey.
Once the bags are packed
By me, and my credit card chimes
Its sweet acceptance, the cashier tells me
"Have a good day!"
I never know exactly what to say
In return. I used to say "You too,"
But can you have a good day
Standing, scanning groceries under
Fluorescent lights, announcements
Clogging the air? Maybe I'm projecting
My inability to be a cashier
Onto someone who performs
A cashier's duties with aplomb,
by necessity or choice.
I can't ask that, and so I say
"Thank you; you as well."
I smile and nod. I return my credit card
To its shy protective sleeve and pivot

To do battle with the metal cart across
The giant potholed parking lot,
Skirting the SUVs and trucks that blaze with anger
In the sun. Where did all the trees go?
Right now I just want to get home
To eat the ice cream before it melts into
This new, unwelcome world.

Prelude

My friend, for me you sit patiently
On ragged cotton,
Listening to the past,
Which slouches loose-jointed,
Weary, the uncomfortable guest.
I empty out
My pockets of their memories,
Stuffed like bones and melon rinds
Into the bulge of years:
Those conversations caught
Against a certain shadow,
A too-insistent sun;
That uncompleted kiss,
Hovering forever
Against the eyes;
Certain hours jostled
Into prominence,
Like awkward children
Trying to explain.
Through it all, you remain
In the important position:
Being there.

Hopeful

I remember we were hopeful
when we bought that yellow house.
We picked it only for its yard, for the overflowing lilacs,
ancient dark-pink rhododendrons, boysenberry bushes
with drooping berries sweet as candy.
Who would willingly choose a house
with scuffed and battered floors
warped by cat and dog piss, a stove caked with dirt,
wallpaper forever unremovable from the walls?
We painted over them and hoped for the best.
Fuses blew their hearts out night and day.
Everything needed
to be repaired or replaced.
We were young and poor, climbing into
a housing market bubble, falling fast and landing
hard on that landlocked yellow cape. It was all
we could afford.
"We will fix you bit by bit," we told it,
and we did. We finally moved
because we couldn't fix
the neighbor on one side.
He hated us. We never learned why.
When leaves from our maple trees blew onto
his lawn, he tossed those leaves right back to ours.
When storms flung lilac branches on his grass,
he kicked those branches back.
One year he cut a massive root
from a boysenberry bush that had the temerity
to wander under the fence

and curl up on his side. I watched, amazed,
as he dug fast as a dog with a bone.
Years later, after we moved, we learned that
he was dead. For a moment I thought I should feel
the tiniest bit sorry for him,
but I didn't feel a thing. I only wondered
if the plants still overflowed the yard, and if they ever,
like me, finally became themselves.

Love Poem

Your laugh walks through
My bones

Your fingers
Braid my nerves

You are the unexploded
Bomb I hold

I didn't ask
For this

Morning Colors

for my uncle Robert, who liked this poem best

I am knee-deep
In morning, looped
By a blue so bright
It strains
Against the windows.

Juice flames
In my glass,
Butter bursts
On a black pan
Like corn
Punching through the soil,
And the sun rises
On the fence
Like so much yeast.

I split a minute
And lick it
From my fingers.

Return Migration

for my parents, who never left the city

I

All days spill
Toward home. All selves
Accompany the return.

Veteran of an unpublished war,
I circulate names and places
For which there are
No echoes and no files;
Yet the ground is buried
Under flesh and brick,
The market crammed
With yeasty faces.

II

I carry my old selves
With me.
          Returning,
We are well advised
To detain the past
Within our pockets and cup it
In our palms, lest it
Sting us in the dark
and demand
What we don't have
To give.

Child, student,
Homeless witch
With greasy shopping bags,
To go home is to live in the draft
Of the selves we were.

III

Old men shuffle
On corners. Their wives drown
In the thin winter sun.
Those who stay
Must have the temperament
For paradise.

Home, all selves
Are wounds. We who return
Blot the city with our tears
Until the streets swim.
Afterwards, we clarify it
With words.

I write the past
Down to the minute
Parts: brows and lashes
On the page, stealing words
To learn the differences
Between them.

Don't Eat the Chicken

for my maternal grandparents

"Don't eat the chicken in a restaurant,"
My skinny angry grandpa warns me,
Speaking too loudly,
Gripping my left hand hard
As we cross the avenue
For Sunday pancakes
On thick white plates,
Three enormous soggy circles
Crowned with melted butter.
"They cook the chicken in gasoline,"
My grandpa says, looking left
Then right for cars that could hit us.
Last week he told me never
To answer the door, "no matter who
They say it is."
My round gentle grandma, on my right side,
Shushes him, as she does each week.
"She's only five, don't scare her,
She doesn't eat out
Except with us for pancakes
When she sleeps over!
She doesn't answer the door—
She can't even reach the chain!
Why do you fill her head with your worries?"
"I'm not worried, Grandma," I say.
And I'm not. I'm curious like the cat.
"Is the oil like the gasoline
Daddy pumps in our car

That's always breaking down,
Or another kind of gasoline
That cooks use to cook?"
My grandmother sighs and tells me that the oil is
Neither, just oil, like the oil she and my mother put
On salads, but maybe not as fresh as our oil at home,
Because restaurants make lots of salads each day
And we make only one. I nod.
I don't want to tell them
That I do eat out. When I have a nickel
I buy a chocolate bar at the corner store
And eat it slowly, square by melting square.
"Don't worry, Grandpa," I say.
Why does he worry so much?
"I promise I won't eat the chicken that's cooked
In gasoline, and I won't answer the door."
He sniffs and harrumphs, and then he quickly runs
His left hand over my hair. In my family,
Worry is always cooked into love.

Gratis

for my two grandmothers

Burps are funny,
And hiccups can set a record,
But mostly our
Cracks, tics, and twitches
Of bone and nerve
Pass unnoticed or ignored.
Only a sneeze, that stoppage
Of the heart, evokes
A blessing.

I have been blessed by friends
And strangers,
By old and young,
Fat and thin,
Inside, outside, day and night,
But only my grandmothers,
Forever knitting,
Worked the words
Into their stitches.

"Knit one, purl two, Gesundheit,"
They said, and said again,
Needles clicking without end.

Toward the End

Toward the end she stopped doing
Much of anything, just cried and cursed
The aides, accused them of stealing
Her dying plants, shrunken socks, unused dentures,
Unwrapped candy, photos taped
Against the wall, pages torn
From envelopes sent sailing through the air.
What she wanted was her youth, life, health—
To be the one who baked a dozen loaves of bread
Most days and gave them all away.
Holding the newspaper was the only thing
That calmed her, so the aides learned
To tuck it right between her elbow
And the chair. Once she sensed its presence
By her side, she smiled.
I remember when she read that paper
Front to back each morning,
Waiting for the loaves to rise.

Shadow Child

We remember you
Each winter
On the day you were scheduled
To arrive, but you had other plans:
To travel from the moment
Of conception through this world
To another place to live.
Only you know your name,
Your sex, the color of your hair and eyes.
We mourn you forever
Without saying a word.

Photograph of a Friend

You're caught in summer, morning.
I can hear the sea.
You've leaned back casually
Against the sand,
Hair mussed, eyes wide, a smile.
I touch your cheek thoughtfully,
As if someone could see me,
Here.

Too large for my wallet,
I've propped you in my kitchen
To watch me wait
As water boils, coffee drips,
Sun rises. You smile at me forever
From a place I never saw
In a day I never spent.
I thank you
For this present.

Plate-Cup-Bowl

This plate, cup, and bowl
Are stamped Less is Enough.
I wanted to give you more,

But like children
Who demand
More toys, more

Hugs and kisses,
You and I want more
Than a body can hold.

We are learning
How much we need
To learn ourselves.

If my gift will hold
Your day, it is more
Than enough.

On Being Yellow

The stick of summer butter
Fills its bar
With the same high
Intensity of color,
And the rose breathes
Yellow in and out
Until it dies.

Dear Jerry

Terry Finch of England posts a 2/3-mile-long letter to
her boyfriend in Texas

She told him all
The big news:
Mum had gone to hospital
For her stomach,
Kathy married
Her jolly grocer,
Derek failed math,
And German,
And gym.

And when there was
No more big news
She wrote
About the price
Of curtains
And the snippy dark-haired
Shopgirl at Boots
And the cute bobby
At the Piccadilly Station

And when there was
No more small news
She wrote
How much
She loved him
And how much

She missed him
And how she couldn't wait
Until they lived
In their own house,
Spreading jam on toast
And watching the water boil
In silence.

Contour Drawing

for David

Though you are beautiful
Enough for me
In motion,

I hunt the delicate
Line of your bones
At rest,

So I may draw the fine
Outline of your hands
Through mine.

On the Hill

All morning the sky
Smooths fresh snow
On your brow,
Tousling trees.

You are white
And solemn,
Draped in confirmation cloth.

Even sound
Wears gloves here
And is dazzled mute.

Only we stand out,
Bright gashes cut
Between road and sky,

Coming to hunt spring,
Chipping for its ribs
Under winter.

Touched Wood

I would arrive
Just as the sky dipped
Its darkened fingers
In the pond and stroked
The clear green water black--
Spun off the last spool
Of light onto the graveled road—
And I would run
From the baggage
Spilling from the trunk
Past the scraps and crumbs
Of travel, the chores.
The house, the waiting arms,
Until I reached
the wharf, rubbed smooth
As sand beneath my feet,
Wood brushed soft as hands
Against my skin,
Old wood, patched wood,
Sanded, softened,
Touched wood.

Reconstitution

Chilly cylinders of juice
Demand three cups of water

And a spoon.
Gallons blossom from the can.

Surely life can be
Reconstituted thus?

Dilution is no less
Than we deserve:

All frozen parts,
Suited for success,

Wait only to be
Liquefied and stirred.

Transformations

To libraries and librarians

I want to be a library.
Not complete,

Not remote and sullen,
But open to improvement

And additions
Of bruised leather,

Creased cardboard,
Loose sheets,

Questionable taste.
Berryman sidling up to Dickinson,

His beard tickling her neck.
Billy and Lord Jim swapping tales.

Eliot and Whitman stiffly spine to spine,
Softening just enough to talk a little

About Camden and St. Louis
Without guilt or gilt.

Typing Papers

Above the windows
And the cracked ceiling,
One floor above my room,
A dull tapping filters
Down.

The rain splatters
On the windows.
My roommate
Puts some water
Up to boil.

The tapping permeates the
House: Henry James
And Walt Whitman,
Trapped in a dual dance
Of maddened keys.

Upstate Spring

You run up with one bag
Three steps at a time,
Leaving the other one balanced

In the wind. Today each slat
Glows a little redder
In the April sun.

The door swings open
Like an anxious lover, waiting
For you to leap down.

Verbal Silences

There are always things
Better left unsaid
Between two people,
For words are often clumsy—
They fumble, hang back, shuffle
Their meanings
On a bashful tongue,
Crumble.

How could I tell you
Out loud
That for me
You are as necessary
as hot, strong coffee
In a blue-glazed pottery mug,
Cupped between cold hands
On a sunny winter morning?

Where the Kissing Never Stops

Before curves kiss,
They have to get acquainted:
Discuss their known
And unknown functions,
Settle a discrete problem or two,
Decide on a common border.

They strive to make each other
Equal zero,
To reach that point
At which they will reduce to lines
And kiss.

They linger
At the intersection of multiplicity,
Although the relationship has been clarified,
The performance rated,
The equation ended.

Greensleeves

My car, Greensleeves, is twenty-three, older than I was
when I drove my first car, Sam.
My grandfather died and left Sam
to me. Sam, a cream sedan dappled with rust,
did not have air-conditioning, power steering,
or power brakes, but the radio worked fine.
After Sam died, no car felt special until I fell in love
with Greensleeves. A cool silvery green,
he has a compact disc player, and my parents,
too long gone, rode in the back seat when they were old
and he was new. I never know when
they'll show up and stay awhile, as long as I don't
turn around, but it's usually when I play
the piano concertos or piano trios of Rachmaninoff.
All three are buried near each other
in that massive cemetery
named for the hall of slain warriors.
They're all heroes, although not one of them knows that
the others are there. Still, I know they're together.
When I drive Greensleeves, a CD playing,
and my parents
behind me, coaxing me forward—
My parents, who loved Rachmaninoff's music;
Rachmaninoff, who loved music;
Greensleeves, whom I named for a song—
I tell Greensleeves to play music and to live
forever, since no one else ever can.

A Walnut Tree

If I were to visit
Your mother's grave, which I will

Never do, I would plant on it
A walnut tree.

No flowers for her, no lush honeyed scents,
No soft petals, no love.

For my own mother I would plant peonies,
Honeysuckle, viburnum, forsythia,

Every wild expressive plant she cherished,
But I can only put a pebble on my mother's grave.

When I do, I tell her that her favorite plants
Are in my garden.

I tell her that I think of her before,
After, and whenever they bloom.

While you grew up your mother worked
Downtown, in women's fashion.

She didn't need the money.
She wanted to be somewhere other

Than home and you. Always she stayed late
For inventory, returning flushed, victorious,

Snapping, "Fix yourself some food, don't bother me
With homework, I'm a career woman, not a loser

Like Betty at the switchboard or Dottie walking
Timmy home from school."

You loved your aunts, how they put their arms
Around you, how they gave you

Plates of cookies on your birthday, always
Topped with powdered sugar soft as clouds.

Your mother didn't bake. She sneered
And tipped the homemade cookies in the trash.

Nothing grows near a walnut tree.
Nothing grew near your mother.

At sixteen, you left home.
Later, your stepfather followed.

Now that your mother is dead,
I take her inventory.

She was empty.
I will never visit her grave.

Midas in His Attic Room

In the modest city in which your father lived,
If a life like his can be called
Living, he took advantage
Of everyone and nothing.
On weekends he stayed inside,
Clipping coupons in his attic
Room, the room he rented hastily
When ejected by his fifth wife's teenage son,
For being cheap and mean.
"My mother buys the food you eat
And pays the mortgage too!
She asks you only
To bring food for dinner,
And what do you bring her, big man
With your government job?
Half-priced loaves of day-old bread?
She doesn't need someone
Like you! Get out!"
Now Midas rents this one small room
Under a low roof, blurred window
Looking out to nowhere,
Scarred pine floor, unfinished walls.
He shuffles coupons and counts his money
Like a king. There will be no new wife,
No talking to his sisters or his sons,
No friends, no love, nothing
But the clanging, crumpled money
In his hands.

Into the City

For my father, the extraordinary city planner

I am traveling into the city you helped
zone, after the war they called the war
to end all wars.

At work each day you asked yourself
questions. Will these buildings
block out too much light?

Can people still walk easily between
school and park, store and train, library and home?
Where will a supermarket fit?

What will make this neighborhood thrive?
Armed with pencils, your team
criss-crossed the boroughs, jotting down

all ideas before returning
to the office with scrawled notes
for next day's morning meeting.

After dinner, I did homework and practiced
the cello. Mom washed dishes and read
the paper, kitchen radio turned on low.

You sat near the phone in the hall and told
the commissioner why some ideas
were better than others.

I think of you as the bus lumbers through
eight horn-choked lanes that convulse to three,
its goal the tunnel to the city.

Through dirty windows I watch cars
forever jockey, no matter time or season.
Who planned this? It wasn't you.

Today I'm here for a concert, although I have
a better reason. I travel here for oxygen,
because isn't where you're born

the place to which you must return?
That's true for me, although I can't
afford to stay or speak for you.

After, I find the old deli, its dim interior
unchanged, its ceiling fans rustling stained paper
menus. "Pastrami sandwich, please," I tell the waiter,
who nods once

and walks away, then rushes back. "On what?"
"On rye, of course."
"I thought you were the bridge-and-tunnel crowd,
wanting different bread."

"No. Always rye. I was born here."
"But now? You live here now?"
I shake my head.

He nods, lips pursed, and brings my sandwich.
I thought I'd always live here, in this city
you helped zone, and it's true I am here

right now, eating my sandwich, napkin
on my lap, program in my bag, bus schedule
carried in my head. I sit in silence

until it's time to go, looking across the booth
where you should be. Passing by,
the waiter sighs, smiles, and leaves the bill.

I Haven't Thought of You

With thanks to Ruthie for sharing her dream

I haven't thought of you
In more than sixty years, but last night
We had sex.
You, team leader at my first job, holding
A half-smoked cigarette between your fingers
While you explain to seventeen new hires
 What the welfare department does.
"We treat each client with respect," you say.
We watch you blow smoke rings upward
Between your words.
You are so handsome in your
Crisp white shirt, dark hair curling
Across your forehead. I think the other girls feel
The same. Now we say women,
But back then we were girls, no matter
How young or old. We wear
Belted dresses, nylons, high heels that pinch
Our toes, our hair sprayed hard into place.
"Stay behind a moment, please," you beckon me
With glowing embers. "Everyone else, please be here
Tomorrow, 9:00 a.m. sharp, prepared to work.
We treat each client with respect. Each person you help
Could someday be you."
"Yes?" I ask, approaching you.
"Is something wrong?"
"Not at all," you say. "I just want to tell you how
Beautiful you are. I want
To sleep with you, but you should know that

I am married. I love my wife and son, and I will never
Leave them. There are so many
Pretty girls here, but you are the prettiest one
I've ever seen. What do you say?"
You take one last puff and grind the butt
With your glossy shoe.
"Well?"
"I say I don't want to sleep with you.
I'm single, yes, but I want my own husband,
And I wouldn't do that to myself or to your wife."
You shrug and turn away.
"Fine. Be here tomorrow, 9 a.m. sharp,
To work, like all the others."
"Yes, sir," I say.
I walk fast enough
To catch up to my friend. She's still waiting
For the bus. It's always late.
"What did he want?" she asks, and I tell her.
"He has a nerve," she says, and I agree.
"He probably tries that with all the new girls."
"I'm sure he succeeds with some, not all."
"We'll never know which ones."
"His poor wife."
We do not think to tell anyone.
We do not think of anyone to tell.
There is no one to tell.
The bus is here, crammed with people hanging
From the straps and pressed against each other
In the muggy air.
We push on and find a narrow place
To stand, swaying with the stops and starts,
Eyes half-closed. I think of nothing else

But getting home
And kicking off my shoes.
My team leader doesn't bother me again.
He treats me exactly like everyone else. I don't know
Whom he asks next, or when he asks again,
Or if he asks at all.
We were all young, or young enough,
And youth is its own beauty. Tie it up
With loneliness and hope, and you'll have
Problems. I think he found someone who said yes.
The next year a shy young man joins
The department and asks me out
On a proper date. He steps inside to meet my parents,
Holding a toy truck for my brother and a hair ribbon
For my sister. He cups my elbow so I don't trip
Over the loose step as we walk down.
"You're so pretty," he says tells me every time
We date. "I want to marry you. Will you marry me?"
"Yes," I say, reaching for his hand. "Yes, I will."
That was long ago. He died last year, after living
A long and mostly happy life. At the end I put
My cheek to his and held the hands of the young man
And the old man until death, impatient,
Pushed my hands away and replaced them
With his own.
Now I'm alone, old
And slow, but I'm still me. Every day
An aide comes, and a nice young man
I've never met rings the bell at noon and leaves
My lunch outside the door.
"Are you OK in there?" he asks, as required.
"Yes, thank you, I am fine," I say.

Once he leaves, I open the door
And get my lunch. Too often now
It's chicken, but I don't complain.
At night, when I can't sleep, I play
The radio and think about
The past. So much is the past.
Last night, again, I dreamed
That I was young, but this time I was
Getting ready for my first job.
I lay out my clothes and waited for the shower
To get hot. I wrapped myself in my favorite
Blue towel and stepped out of
The tub, eyes half-closed, hair dripping.
I hear my mother call me.
"Don't be late for your first day!"
"Yes, Mama, I'll be down for breakfast soon!"
I lean forward to look in the mirror, and there you are, behind me.
We speak no words, but when I turn, you take me
In your arms, and as we kiss
My towel falls away and I press into you until
My eyes open.
That's when I awaken, alone in my bed,
In the apartment of my marriage, startled.
I haven't thought of you in more than sixty years.
Am I responsible for my dreams?

To Keep You in This World

I look for you
The old way, walking

Through a library. I pick up
Books assigned to shelves and tables.

Any one of them
Might contain a bookplate with a name

In memory of,
Like the bookplates I write

When I give money to the library
To buy books for you:

Parent, grandparent, friend,
Cousin, spouse of, neighbor.

It's my way of keeping all of you
Alive, or in this world

If not exactly alive, because
When a book with your name

Is opened, I believe you breathe.
When a book with your name

Is read, you are alive, held by
Someone's hands.

If all books with bookplates
Were read at the same time,

Would your paths cross somewhere
All of you can reach but I cannot?

I'm not convinced you want to be
Here, in this world, even briefly,

But I need to find you
Sometimes, to see

Your names in print, to ask you
Questions, to share jokes

And laugh out loud,
To write the cartoon captions

For contests we will never win.
The bookplate? It's just a small block

Of ivory curlicued with gray,
Like any rough rectangle

Of a sidewalk
In the cities we once walked.

No one sees your name
Without an open book.

Is your name still there
When the book is closed?

Please tell me that it is.
Please tell me you're still here,

In this world, and everywhere my heart
Might find you.

Answers

I waited too long
To ask you questions.
You lie in in the hospital, almost
Gone.

You say they buried the babies
On Roosevelt Island, but what was
Her name, and when was she
Born?

You say you loved the boy on the bike.
Where did you meet him?
Did he love you
Back?

Your answers are forever
Lost inside you.

Consigned

I have consigned clothes for forty years.
Each season I sort through
What to keep and what to let go.
Can I wear this shirt again if I lose
Five pounds? Will this dress come back
In style? Might I suddenly look good in red,
A color that I never wear?
Sometimes I put clothes aside
To ponder later.
Mostly I reach to pin the tag
On which I write my number,
The size, and information
Like material or brand.
Each item is a road between
Where I was and where I am.
Decisions made, I snip an errant thread
From one sweater that's so old
The store on its frayed label
Closed thirty years ago.
When I was young
My mother took me to that store
Each fall to shop for clothes.
Although this sweater is too small,
Pilled, and out of style, I find
I cannot let it go.
What I save, invisible
To all but me, are memories,
Like this cashmere sweater carefully folded
Against my heart, pale wool
Soft as wings against my hands.

Memory Box

When I remember to clean
The house, I find the box
My husband calls my memory box.
Duster on my lap, I sit down and spill

Its papers on the nearest bed. Here
Is my report card from Mrs. Grayson,
My teacher in sixth grade.
She seemed old

But was probably young.
In her fitted blue dress,
Hair puffed into a helmet
With flipped ends, she had

That certain charm of women long ago:
Careful makeup, high heels,
Stockings, a brooch, endless worry
About one's weight and the necessary

Flat stomach, small wristwatch with
Smooth leather band, patterned scarf,
Pearl earrings glinting
In the sun, glossy red lipstick

So lovingly applied.
I see her now.
I never liked her.
I liked Mrs. Golden,

Round as a buttered scone, who taught math.
Once a boy asked Mrs. Grayson to spell
"Institute," and all the girls held their breath,
Afraid she would say "tit," but she broke

The word into three syllables
Without missing a beat, smiling at the class
As the boys groaned and the girls relaxed.
She wrote that I had good days

And bad days and that I was capable
Of doing better even on good days.
"She talks too much to her friends
Instead of listening."

"Can we have lunch now?" my husband calls.
"Yes, I'll make us sandwiches," I call back.
I bend down to slide Mrs. Grayson into the box
And the box under the bed.

All That Time

My doctor says
"Remember these words: dog, grass, ball."
Right away I see a golden dog, a small red ball
Between his paws, his wet nose nuzzling
It forward, on grass so green it hurts my eyes.
I'm afraid I'll forget the words before the doctor
Asks me to repeat them, so I repeat them to myself
While she keeps talking, her questions muffled,
Floating through my head.
"Are these the medicines you take?"
I nod. She knows they are
Because she's reading from a list.
"Any injuries or hospitalizations this past year?"
I shake my head no. I am careful to hold on
To the bannister, avoid the cracked sidewalk,
Wear the ugly shoes
With good tread. This morning I stood before
The cupboard, wondering why I opened it,
Until I remembered I already ate my oatmeal.
"Now tell me those three words," she says, and I do.
"Very good! Please give this paper to the front desk
On your way out,
And we'll see you in one year. Call sooner
If you have a problem. Don't ever hesitate to call."
When she says "call" I see a phone, an old phone,
A black rotary phone, the phone of my childhood.
"This is how you dial,"
My so-young mother showed me,
Guiding my hand.

"The 9 and the 0 take too long!" I complained.
"The small numbers go faster. I want
All the numbers to go fast, like 1 and 2 and 3."
Now I want all that time, my young mother, and more.

Water

Can we seniors be forgiven for thinking that
Gush, spurt, dribble, and stream could
Mean water, the clear turquoise water
Of our youth, when we lay poolside
Or on rocks, warmed
By lust and sun, our hands touching
Each other, not holding
A box of incontinence pads
Up to our reading glasses to see
The fine print?

Tee Shirts

I dislike online
Shopping, so I must walk or drive

To look for ordinary
Tee shirts, tee shirts once sold

Everywhere, solid colors
Of thick cotton, with a ribbed crew neck

And comfortable short sleeves.
Where are those tee shirts now?

There are cheap shirts in some stores,
Scratchy and see-through.

Other stores have more expensive shirts,
Softer but still see-through.

There are stripes, dots, hearts, and prints
With cheery words exhorting me to run and jump.

I want solid tee shirts that don't talk back
To anyone, although I'll accept

Muted color block and tie-dye variations,
Preferably in organic cotton.

Everywhere, grinning salespeople
Surround me like locusts, chattering

"Look at this, it will look so good
On you, it's 40 percent off today only,

Let me start a dressing room,"
and, head hurting, I flee without a word

to a nearby thrift shop and pluck
A clump of shirts from a metal rack

That squeaks and shudders as it spins.
Holding them close, I sit and breathe deeply

In the dressing room for a long time
For the quiet. Then I choose three

Faded, well-washed shirts once worn
By other people in other lives

And buy them, glad my search
Is over for this summer.

A Memory I Didn't Know

A memory I didn't know I had
Sat down with me on Christmas Day
In a diner booth northwest of Philadelphia.
It put its elbows on my table
While I ordered the U-Pick-2.
I chose soup and a half
Sandwich, ignoring the health call
Of salad. Leave that for spring!
Soup is warmer, and I was cold.
That day's sweet and sour
Cabbage soup came to the table
In a heavy white bowl
Of steaming memory
From my grandmother's kitchen.
I was there so often
As a child, elbows pressed
On her table as she ladled soup
Into my bowl and gently moved
Buttered slices of homemade bread
Near my hand.

Step Inside with Me

I'm at the station. Please step inside
This poem with me. Help me
Find my train. There are too many choices.
There are too many tracks.
Long ago I picked the trip
I thought was right and bought my ticket.
Maybe it was right
At that moment, or maybe it was always
Wrong. The train left the station
Ahead of time to reach its destination
Early, that stop I was so sure
I wanted. I was young.
Now, old, I hover just inside
The station, between an entrance and an exit,
Listening to the sounds of choices
I didn't make
Float toward me and away.

Fault

Remember that it is never our fault
When something goes wrong
With technology, as we climb
To the platform
Through the browser
With our mouse
By our side because the trackpad
Is too hard to use.
Something always goes wrong
With technology, with the app
The sound
The camera
The logon
The password,
Or the power goes out
In its old-fashioned way
Because now public utilities
Are owned
By hedge funds
Looking to spin off
Their assets and faulty wiring
To the greediest bidder.

We wait patiently for
A connection to occur, obsessively
Checking to make sure
We have not entered a fake
Website, one keystroke away
From our intended,

And that our personal information
Remains safe. Everything is
Outsourced to everyone, and no one
Is responsible for solving
Any problems
We will experience.
We are prisoners in this
Brave new world we never chose.
Lately I've taken
To bringing a book
Of literary fiction, checked out
From the library, wherever I go.
I read it while waiting
Online, on line, in line,
Because the world I want
To live in exists
In its pages, not on a screen.

Concert

As a child, I heard the subway coming
Long before the train arrived.
Air tightened in my ears.
"I don't know how I know," I told my friends.
"I must just have good hearing."

The city chattered day and night
Beside me, but I loved
Its rhymes and rhythms, percussion
Of metal, thump of tire, serenade of horn, siren
Wailing its mournful song while rounding the corner.

I still don't mind those sounds. They are their own
Music. Fake noise bothers me.
In supermarkets and waiting rooms
I cower, forever dodging the blasts
Of braying television.

But please, do play classical music
For me, especially the Romantic piano pieces
Of the nineteenth century.
When you are done, holding your hands
Over the keys before I clap, I feel
There is nothing as loud and sweet as that moment
Of silence, before the storm of applause.

The Minor Keys

Sometimes I wonder where I'll be
When I am gone. It might be nice
To have my ashes sprinkled
In all the places I remember,
But there's a plot in the family cemetery
Waiting for me.

I don't like those choices, and so I wonder
What to be. I could be a bird,
My hollow bones soaring high above
The world's pain, but I don't have the energy
To fly. What if I'm a book that no one wants
To read?

Besides, I don't want to be alone again.
I want to be with others like me:
Quiet, moody, yearning for endless music
In the minor keys.
Telemann understood E minor to be
"Pensive, profound...expressive of grief,
And deep-thinking."

I could be a cello, I suppose,
Or an oboe, or violin, but I'll always
Choose the piano. I'll be one
Of its eighty-eight keys.
I won't be the sad lowest A or the shrill highest B,
Nor middle C, ubiquitous and too anxious to please.

I'll be huddled above or below,
Slightly off balance, surprising you
With my dissonance and charm.
Look for me near your favorite Chopin intersection
On the nine-foot Steinway concert grand
I once played for a lark but never owned.

The Goodbye Waltz

For my mother, fellow music lover

That Chopin waltz is the only
Piece of music I've ever memorized
Without trying. I know it
Was your favorite, and suddenly
I could play it through
By heart, a few months after
You died. Although my heart was clenched
With loss of you, playing that waltz brought you
Back through the air, to the piano, and to me.
I accepted—or not accepted, became resigned to—
Your absence. Then it became impossible
To play the waltz from memory,
And that smaller loss is another
Disappointment to bear.
I still play it, from the score,
Hoping it will summon you.

Roots

We are entangled in words.
They take root
In our stomachs and branch out
From our lips, sprouting
Through sleep.

No matter what dreams hold us
By the throat, we awaken
With stories in our fingers,
Groping
To plant a poem.

Acknowledgements

Thank you to:

Friends and family who read, commented on, and inspired some of these poems.

Journals that published my poems or sent encouraging rejection letters.

Poet Donald Finkel (1929-2008), for allowing me to study with him for a creative-thesis master's degree at Washington University in St. Louis.

Serving House books, for publishing this collection of poems.

CREDITS

The following poems have appeared elsewhere, sometimes in different versions:

"To Keep You in This World," Spring 2025, *Metonym Journal*

"Hopeful," December 2023, *Constellations*

"Greensleeves" and "All That Time," November 2023, *Volney Road Review*

"Toward the End," "The Minor Keys," and "No Words," Fall 2022, *Plum Creek Review*

"Concert," April 2022, *Wingless Dreamer*

"Beginnings," "High Sail," "Nightmare," "Road Rage," "Cheers," "Summer," "Small Wars," "The Cutting Board," "Winter Day," "Gestures," "On the Roof," "Winter's Wounds," "Mistress Hopkins," "A Day of Hearts," "Clocks and Hearts," "Dream Practice," "Asleep," "Last Thanksgiving," "The Closet," "Hands," "Idling," "Laundry," "Lecture," "Footnote," "Obscene Phone Call," "Prelude," "Love Poem," "Morning Colors," "Return Migration," "Gratis," "Photograph of a Friend," "Plate-Cup-Bowl," "On Being Yellow," "Dear Jerry," "Contour Drawing," "On the Hill," "Touched Wood," "Reconstitution," "Transformations," "Typing Papers," "Upstate Spring," "Verbal Silences," "Where the Kissing Never Stops," and "Roots," March 2020, *Verbal Silences,* Duck Lake Press.

"Where the Kissing Never Stops," 2008, *Strange Attractors* (anthology).

THE AUTHOR

Ann Calandro is a writer, mixed media collage artist, and classical piano student. For many years she worked as a writer and copyeditor in medical publishing, medical communications, and advertising. Her fiction, creative nonfiction, and poetry have been published in literary journals and anthologies. Her artwork has appeared in juried exhibits and literary journals. Shanti Arts Press published three children's books that she wrote and illustrated. In 2025, Serving House Books published her collection of short fiction *Lost in Words*. Born and raised in New York City, Calandro received a master's degree in English from Washington University in St Louis. See her artwork at ann-calandro.pixels.com

www.ingramcontent.com/pod-product-compliance
Lightning Source LLC
Chambersburg PA
CBHW060534080526
44586CB00012B/727

9 781947 175761